SHAKESPEARE'S MACBETH

AN AQA ESSAY WRITING GUIDE

R. P. DAVIS

Copyright © 2020 Accolade Tuition Ltd
Published by Accolade Tuition Ltd
71-75 Shelton Street
Covent Garden
London WC2H 9JQ
www.accoladetuition.com
info@accoladetuition.com

ISBN 978-1-9163735-1-8

FIRST EDITION
1 3 5 7 9 10 8 6 4 2

For Ernest.

CONTENTS

FOREWORD

In your GCSE English Literature exam, you will be presented with an extract from Shakespeare's *Macbeth* and a question that asks you to offer both a close analysis of the extract plus a commentary of the play as a whole. Of course, there are many methods one *might* use to tackle this style of question. However, there is one particular technique which, due to its sophistication, most readily allows students to unlock the highest marks: namely, **the thematic method**.

To be clear, this study guide is *not* intended to walk you through the play scene-by-scene: there are many great guides out there that do just that. No, this guide, by sifting through a series of mock exam questions, will demonstrate *how* to organise a response thematically and thus write a stellar essay: a skill we believe no other study guide adequately covers!

I have encountered students who have structured their essays all sorts of ways: some by writing about the extract line by line, others by identifying various language techniques and giving each its own paragraph. The method I'm advocating, on the other hand, involves picking out three to four themes that will allow you to holistically answer the question: these three to four themes will become the three to four content paragraphs of your essay, cushioned between a brief introduction and conclusion. Ideally, these themes will follow from one to the next to create a flowing argument. Within each of these thematic paragraphs, you can then ensure you are jumping through the mark scheme's hoops.

So to break things down further, each thematic paragraph will include various point-scoring components. In each paragraph, you will quote from the extract, offer analyses of these quotes, then discuss how the specific language techniques you have identified illustrate the theme you're discussing. In each paragraph, you will also discuss how other parts of the play further illustrate the theme (or even complicate it). And in each, you will comment on the era in which the play was written and how that helps to understand the chosen theme.

Don't worry if this all feels daunting. Throughout this guide, I will be illustrating in great detail – by means of examples – how to build an essay of this kind.

The beauty of the thematic approach is that, once you have your themes, you suddenly have a direction and a trajectory, and this makes essay writing a whole lot easier. However, it must also be noted that extracting themes in

The Shakespearian equivalent of a selfie.

the first place is something students often find tricky. I have come across many candidates who understand the extract and the play inside out; but when they are presented with a question under exam conditions, and the pressure kicks in, they find it tough to break their response down into themes. The fact of the matter is: the process is a *creative* one and the best themes require a bit of imagination.

In this guide, I shall take seven different exam-style questions, coupled with extracts from the play, and put together a plan for each – a plan that illustrates in detail how we will be satisfying the mark scheme's criteria. Please do keep in mind that, when operating under timed conditions, your plans will necessarily be less detailed than those that appear in this volume.

Now, you might be asking whether three or four themes is best. The truth is, you should do whatever you feel most comfortable with: the examiner is looking for an original, creative answer, and not sitting there counting the themes. So if you think you are quick enough to cover four, then great. However, if you would rather do three to make sure you do each theme justice, that's also fine. I sometimes suggest that my student pick four themes, but make the fourth one smaller – sort of like an afterthought, or an observation that turns things on their head. That way, if they feel they won't have time to explore this fourth theme in its own right, they can always give it a quick mention in the conclusion instead.

The Globe Theatre in London. It was built on the site of the original, which was burnt down in 1613.

Before I move forward in earnest, I believe it to be worthwhile to run through the four Assessment Objectives the exam board want you to cover in your response – if only to demonstrate how effective the thematic response can be. I would argue that the first Assessment Objective (AO1) – the one that wants candidates to 'read, understand and respond to texts' and which is worth 12 of the total 34 marks up for grabs – will be wholly satisfied by selecting strong themes, then fleshing them out with quotes. Indeed, when it comes to identifying the top-scoring candidates for AO1, the mark scheme explicitly tells examiners to look for a 'critical, exploratory, conceptualised response' that makes 'judicious use of precise references' – the word 'concept' is a synonym of theme, and 'judicious references' simply refers to quotes that appropriately support the theme you've chosen.

The second Assessment Objective (AO2) – which is also responsible for 12 marks – asks students to 'analyse the language, form and structure used by a writer to create meanings and effects, using relevant subject terminology where appropriate.' As noted, you will already be quoting from the play as you back up your themes, and it is a natural progression to then analyse the language techniques used. In fact, this is far more effective than simply observing language techniques (personification here, alliteration there), because by discussing how the language techniques relate to and shape the theme, you will also be demonstrating how the writer 'create[s] meanings and effects.'

Now, in my experience, language analysis is the most important element of AO2 – perhaps 8 of the 12 marks will go towards language analysis. You will also notice, however, that AO2 asks students to comment on 'form and structure.' Again, the thematic approach has your back – because though simply jamming in a point on form or structure will feel jarring, when you bring these points up while discussing a theme, as a means to further a thematic argument, you will again organically be discussing the way it 'create[s] meanings and effects.'

AO3 requires you to 'show understanding of the relationships between texts and the contexts in which they were written' and is responsible for a more modest 6 marks in total. These are easy enough to weave into a thematic argument; indeed, the theme gives the student a chance to bring up context in a relevant and fitting way. After all, you don't want it to look like you've just shoehorned a contextual factoid into the mix.

Finally, you have AO4 – known also as "spelling and grammar." There are four marks up for grabs here. Truth be told, this guide is not geared towards AO4. My advice? Make sure you are reading plenty of books and articles, because the more you read, the better your spelling and grammar will be. Also, before the exam, perhaps make a list of words you struggle to spell but often find yourself using in essays, and commit them to memory.

| The Globe Theatre's interior.

My hope is that this book, by demonstrating how to tease out themes from an extract, will help you feel more confident in doing so yourself. I believe it is also worth mentioning that the themes I have picked out are by no means definitive. Asked the very same question, someone else may pick out different themes, and write an answer that is just as good (if not better!). Obviously the exam is not likely to be fun – my memory of them is pretty much the exact opposite. But still, this is one of the very few chances that you will get at GCSE level to actually be creative. And to my mind at least, that was always more enjoyable – if *enjoyable* is the right word – than simply demonstrating that I had memorised loads of facts.

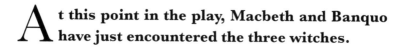

At this point in the play, Macbeth and Banquo have just encountered the three witches.

MACBETH

[Aside] Two truths are told,
As happy prologues to the swelling act
Of the imperial theme.--I thank you, gentlemen.
[Aside] This supernatural soliciting
Cannot be ill, cannot be good: if ill,
Why hath it given me earnest of success,
Commencing in a truth? I am thane of Cawdor:
If good, why do I yield to that suggestion
Whose horrid image doth unfix my hair
And make my seated heart knock at my ribs,
Against the use of nature? Present fears
Are less than horrible imaginings:
My thought, whose murder yet is but fantastical,
Shakes so my single state of man that function
Is smother'd in surmise, and nothing is
But what is not.

Starting with this extract, write about how Shakespeare portrays the supernatural.

Write about:

- how Shakespeare portrays the supernatural in this extract

- how Shakespeare portrays the supernatural in the play as a whole

Introduction

It's important to keep the introduction short and sweet, but also to ensure it packs a punch – after all, you only have one chance to make a first impression on the examiner. I recommend starting the introduction with a short comment on historical context to score early AO3 marks. I would then suggest that you very quickly summarize the thematic gist of your essay.

In this instance, I score early AO3 marks by invoking a titbit of history that places *Macbeth* in context. After this, I keep things short and sweet, hinting at the approach I am about to take.

"Given that Shakespeare's England was a place preoccupied with the supernatural –indeed, Elizabeth I even went so far as to pass a Witchcraft Act in 1592, outlawing 'Conjurations' – it is little surprise that such phenomena permeate his plays. Macbeth's reaction to the witches in this extract not only highlights the sexualisation of the supernatural and the deep ambivalence it induces, but also points to its capacity to galvanise."[1]

Theme/Paragraph One: Shakespeare presents Macbeth's encounter with the witches – the play's chief supernatural entities – as something sordid, sleazy and even sexual.

- The sibilant phrase 'supernatural soliciting' that Macbeth deploys to characterise the witches' words is striking: the word 'soliciting' contains resonances of prostitution, as if to imply that the witches – like prostitutes – were attempting to pedal sordid sexual services. It also lends the witches a Faustian dimension: Macbeth can have what he desires, but only if he is willing to pay a moral price.[2] [*AO1 for advancing the argument with a judiciously selected quote; AO2 for the close analysis of the language*].
- When approached with a Freudian eye, the description of Macbeth's physical state in this extract further reinforces the idea his encounter with the witches had an almost sexual dimension.[3] Although Macbeth protests that the encounter was 'horrid,' the primitivity with which he describes his physical response is reminiscent of sexual arousal: '[it] doth unfix my hair / And make my seated heart knock at my ribs.' That the phrase 'knock at my ribs' constitutes two inverted, spondaic feet emphasises Macbeth's physical disarray: the metre mimics his hammering, excited heart.[4] One might note that the superstitious Jacobean audience believed not only that the voices of witches took a devastating toll on a listener, but also

that a woman's voice was physically linked to her sexual organs.[5] [*AO2 for the close analysis of the language; AO3 for invoking historical context that deepens our understanding of the text*].

- *Elsewhere in the play*: In the passage just before this extract, the witches' own words draw attention to their sexually charged nature. The First Witch talks about following a sailor to Aleppo, a passage that ends with 'I'll do, I'll do, I'll do' – a clear allusion to fornication.

Theme/Paragraph Two: The supernatural induces deep ambivalence – and doubt – in those who encounter it.

- Macbeth is at once both excited by the witches' predictions, yet also repulsed by them. This paradoxical sentiment is captured in his verdict that their words, 'cannot be good, cannot be ill.' Indeed, the use of litotes here – Macbeth rhetorically avoids labelling the witches' words outright as 'good' and 'ill' – further accentuates his uncertain state of mind.[6] [*AO1 for advancing the argument with a judiciously selected quote; AO2 for the close analysis of the language*].

- Macbeth interrogates both the 'ill' and 'good' sensations the 'supernatural soliciting' induces in him, and finds reason to doubt both. Interestingly, Macbeth's ambivalence extends to the thoughts of murder that the supernatural predictions have inspired. The very fact he alludes to murder in this soliloquy implicitly communicates a desire to carry it out, whereas his visceral reaction to the idea – it 'shakes so [his] single state of man' – communicates his disgust. [*AO2 for the close analysis of the language*].

- *Elsewhere in the play*: One might draw a contrast with Macbeth's encounter with Banquo's ghost later in the play. On that occasion, Macbeth's reaction is not ambivalent; it is characterised by full-blown horror: 'look on that / Which might appal the devil.'

Theme/Paragraph Three: Shakespeare presents the witches, and the supernatural forces they embody, as an affront to, and an inversion of, the natural order.

- Although when Macbeth uses the phrase 'against the use of nature' he is talking about his pounding heart, it is not unreasonable to construe that phrase also as a hint of Macbeth's understanding of the supernatural entities who have set his heart racing. The witches represent a force that is at odds with – or even antagonistic to – the natural order of things. To Macbeth's mind, the supernatural is also *anti*-natural. [*AO1 for advancing the argument with a judiciously selected quote; AO2 for the close analysis of the language*].

- The soliloquy's final sentiment – 'Nothing is / but what is not' – implies that the only things that exist are those things that do *not* exist, and is a testament to how the witches have turned the natural order inside out. The line break after 'is' constitutes an effective use of form: the pause it encourages ensures that there is a brief verbal nothingness to mirror the 'nothingness' under discussion. [*AO2 for observing how form shapes meaning*].

- *Elsewhere in the play*: The idea that the witches are at odds with the natural order is encapsulated by the phrase 'fair is foul and foul is fair,' which the witches speak in the play's opening scene, and which rhetorically conjures a universe in which the natural order has been inverted, and good has become bad and vice versa. The structural choice of placing this at the very end of Act 1, Scene 1, allows it to function almost as an epigraph, delineating how the supernatural will make itself felt throughout the play.[7] [*AO2 for observing how structure shapes meaning*].

Theme/Paragraph Four: Shakespeare portrays the witches, and their supernatural predictions, as a force that inspires action in other characters and drives the narrative.

- By making their predictions that Macbeth shall be King ('Macbeth, thou shalt be king hereafter'), the witches inspire Macbeth to follow down the path to murdering Duncan; indeed, that he is thinking along those lines is already evident in this passage: 'whose murder yet is but fantastical.' [*AO1 for advancing the argument with a judiciously selected quote*].
- *Elsewhere in the play*: Later in the play, the words of the witches' equivocating apparition – that 'Macbeth shall never vanquish'd be until / Great Birnam wood [shall come] to high Dunsinane hill' – again galvanises Macbeth down a certain course of action: namely, his hubristic last stand at his castle at Dunsinane Hill.

Conclusion

I have covered all the themes I was hoping to in the paragraphs above. As a result, I will first make reference to another Shakespeare play in a bid to mop up any remaining AO3 marks going spare. Then, in a final AO1-scoring flourish, I will wrap things up with a brief parting comment that captures the essay's central argument.

"If, in Hamlet's words, 'there are more things in heaven and earth, Horatio / than are dreamt of in your philosophy,' the play *Macbeth* is a deep-dive into such 'things.'[8] However, whereas the supernatural in *Hamlet* is shot-through with masculinity (the ghost is Hamlet's father), the fact the central supernatural entities in *Macbeth* are female opens up themes regarding transgressive sexuality. There is also, arguably, a greater deal of subtlety in *Macbeth*, populated as it is with spectral presences like Act 5's 'Seyton' – perhaps just a servant, perhaps a symbol of the 'supernatural soliciting['s]' ubiquity."[9]

A poster for Thomas W. Keene's 1884
production of *Macbeth*.

A t this point in the play, Duncan has arrived at Macbeth castle.

LADY MACBETH

Come, you spirits
That tend on mortal thoughts, unsex me here,
And fill me from the crown to the toe top-full
Of direst cruelty! make thick my blood;
Stop up the access and passage to remorse,
That no compunctious visitings of nature
Shake my fell purpose, nor keep peace between
The effect and it! Come to my woman's breasts,
And take my milk for gall, you murdering ministers,
Wherever in your sightless substances
You wait on nature's mischief! Come, thick night,
And pall thee in the dunnest smoke of hell,
That my keen knife see not the wound it makes,
Nor heaven peep through the blanket of the dark,
To cry 'Hold, hold!'

Starting with this passage, discuss the extent to which Shakespeare portrays Lady Macbeth as a strong character.

Write about:

• **how Shakespeare presents Lady Macbeth as a strong character in this extract**

• **how Shakespeare presents Lady Macbeth as a strong character in the play as a whole**

Introduction

As I have suggested before, we want to start with an early AO3 point; then we want to follow up with a quick nod to the themes you have in mind.

"At the heart of turn of the seventeenth century life was a paradox: women were ubiquitously subjugated to patriarchal structures that insisted they be married-off and subservient, yet the head of state up until 1603 was the unrepentantly non-conformist (and unmarried) Queen Elizabeth. Lady Macbeth, a woman hungry to elevate herself to head-of-state status, draws strength in self-consciously rejecting femininity and the submissiveness it implies; however, she is ultimately weakened by her surfeit of ambition."

Theme/Paragraph One: Shakespeare, by having Lady Macbeth forcefully abdicate her femininity and womanhood in this passage, portrays her as self-consciously rejecting the submissiveness demanded from women.

- The association of femininity with weakness was ingrained in the Elizabethan and Jacobean psyche: the words Hamlet levels at Ophelia – 'Frailty thy name is woman' – powerfully captures the prevailing societal perception. Lady Macbeth is attempting to purge herself of that womanhood in this passage as she calls upon spirits to 'unsex me here.' However, Lady Macbeth takes this abdication further when she exhorts these spirits to 'Come to my woman's breasts, / And take my milk for gall.' A mother's milk is a uniquely gendered substance that ties women to child-rearing and calls to mind an urge to nurture. As a result, by wishing away her 'milk,' Lady Macbeth seeks to renounce the biological imperative to nurture, since she deems it at odds with the violence required to realise her ambitions. [*AO1 for advancing the argument with a judiciously selected quote; AO2 for the close analysis of the language; AO3 for bringing in another text that helps us understand the play in the wider cultural milieu*].

- Lady Macbeth also alliteratively invokes a knife – 'my keen knife' – and in the scenes that follow, she is instrumental in selecting the knife as the weapon by which the Duncan's murder shall be carried out. Seen through a Freudian lens, Lady Macbeth's close association with this phallic object suggests that she has not only renounced her womanhood, but that she has actively sought to appropriate traits stereotypically associated with manhood – violence, dominance, physical strength. By having Lady Macbeth flout contemporary gender expectations, Shakespeare endows her with a kind of raw strength usually reserved for men. [*AO2 for the close analysis of the language; AO3 for invoking historical context that deepens our understanding of the text*].

Theme/Paragraph Two: Lady Macbeth's willingness to use language associated with war and physical violence lends her a rhetorical strength – since *Macbeth* is a play in which violence and warring is tightly linked to the brokering of power.

- Lady Macbeth's soliloquy here is littered with imagery that brings to mind war and physical violence. Lady Macbeth refers to her 'fell purpose' – the word 'fell' is evocative of the act of striking down – and she is anxious not to experience any guilt that might lead her to 'keep peace:' the jarring half-rhyme between 'keep' and 'peace' reflecting the discord Lady Macbeth wishes to sow. Indeed, as the passage progresses, the violent imagery becomes all the more explicit: Lady Macbeth talks in blunt terms about 'the wound' her 'keen knife' will make. [*AO1 for advancing the argument with a judiciously selected quote; AO2 for the close analysis of the language*].
- *Elsewhere in the play*: Lady Macbeth proves that her love-affair with violence is not merely verbal: she is

the one who drugs Duncan's guards and pushes Macbeth to take Duncan's life. Lady Macbeth does indeed gain the crown through this use of violence, illustrating that violence does directly correlate with the accrual of power within the play. This violent coup reflects the tumult of Shakespeare's England: for instance, in 1601 – shortly before *Macbeth* was written – the Earl of Essex tried (and failed) to seize power from Queen Elizabeth. [*AO3 for invoking historical context that deepens our understanding of the text*].

Theme/Paragraph Three: Lady Macbeth's language in this soliloquy is reminiscent of a witch's spell: she is invoking dark forces to help her achieve her aims. This links her to the three powerful women that appear intermittently throughout the play – the witches – who cast a spell on Macbeth, and control everyone's fate.

- This extract is deeply reminiscent in tone to a witch's spell. The opening line attempts to conjure a supernatural entity that might assist Lady Macbeth – 'Come, you spirits' – and the structural choice of placing this invocation at the soliloquy's start ensures that everything that follows is imbued with an air of incantation. [*AO1 for advancing the argument with a judiciously selected quote; AO2 for observing how structure shapes meaning*].
- This attempt to open a dialogue with transcendent forces persists throughout the passage: Lady Macbeth calls upon 'murdering ministers' – the alliteration

redoubling the sense of an incantation – and then 'thick night' itself, as though 'thick night' were a personified, supernatural entity. [*AO2 for the close analysis of the language*].

- This lends Lady Macbeth a kind of strength, since it links her intimately to the witches: the supernatural entities who exert control over the fate of the entire Dramatis Personae.[1] Indeed, in Act 4 Scene 1, the witches actually conjure apparitions – a seeming literalisation of the sort of incantation Lady Macbeth is engaging in here.

Conclusion

As it so happens, I have one final theme up my sleeve; however, because the essay is already quite a healthy length, I shall explore the final theme briefly as I wrap things up, and score some last-minute AO1 marks in doing so:

"It ought to be observed that in a key way, however, Lady Macbeth is in fact presented as weak in this passage: she seems to be a slave to her ambitions. Indeed, the litany of exclamation marks throughout the passage seem to connote a heightened emotional state that arguably indicates that her ambitions have sent her spinning out of control. However, while Lady Macbeth's ambition does eventually lead to her downfall – it 'o'erleaps itself,' to borrow Macbeth's phrase – it undeniably also makes her a formidable force in the first place."

A statue of Lady Macbeth in Stratford-upon-Avon, the town in which Shakespeare was born.

READ THE FOLLOWING EXTRACT FROM
ACT 1 SCENE 7 OF MACBETH AND
ANSWER THE QUESTION THAT
FOLLOWS.

A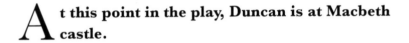t this point in the play, Duncan is at Macbeth
castle.

MACBETH
Prithee, peace.
I dare do all that may become a man;
Who dares do more is none.
LADY MACBETH
What beast was't then
That made you break this enterprise to me?
When you durst do it, then you were a man.
And to be more than what you were, you would
Be so much more the man. Nor time, nor place
Did then adhere, and yet you would make both.
They have made themselves and that their fitness now
Does unmake you. I have given suck and know
How tender 'tis to love the babe that milks me:
I would, while it was smiling in my face,
Have plucked my nipple from his boneless gums
And dashed the brains out, had I so sworn

As you have done to this.

Starting with this extract, how does Shakespeare present temptation in the play?

Write about:

• **how Shakespeare presents temptation in this extract**

• **how Shakespeare presents temptation in the play as a whole**

Introduction

As ever, my first sentence scores AO3 (contextual) marks; and my second sentence broaches the AO1 ideas the essay will explore.

"At the turn of the seventeenth century, the concept of temptation would have been seen through the prism of Christian orthodoxy: to Shakespeare's deeply religious audience, temptation would have chiefly brought to mind the seduction of Adam and Eve in Genesis.[1] In this passage, Lady Macbeth becomes a pseudo-Eve, tempting Macbeth to adopt her regicidal mindset.[2] In dramatising this process, Shakespeare frames temptation as a sexualised force, fuelled by powerful rhetoric."

Theme/Paragraph One: Shakespeare in this passage presents Lady Macbeth – and, by extension, temptation – as a persistent force that cannibalizes the logic that attempts to rebuff it.

- This passage in fact starts with Macbeth declining to kill Duncan, and arguing that doing so would reduce him to nothing: 'Who dares do more is none.' However, temptation is portrayed as a persistent force that does not take no for an answer: Lady Macbeth immediately taunts Macbeth for his comment and seeks to take his logic and invert it. Whereas Macbeth argues that killing Duncan would make him no longer a man, Lady Macbeth argues that it would in fact make him 'so much more the man.' [*AO1 for advancing the argument with a judiciously selected quote*].

- One might observe that when Macbeth attempts to nix the idea with a line containing three metrical feet – 'Who dares do more is none' – Lady Macbeth in fact completes the iambic pentameter with the first line of her reply, which contains two further metrical feet: 'What beast was't then.' This use of form here reflects how temptation sinks its teeth into the logic seeking to neutralise it, before weaponizing it against itself. [*AO2 for observing how form shapes meaning*].

- *Elsewhere in the play*: Whereas Lady Macbeth does battle with Macbeth's logic in order to fan the flames of his desire, the witches – the other key engines of temptation – use a different tactic. In Act 1 Scene 2, when the witches float the notion that Macbeth will be Thane of Cawdor, Macbeth attempts to dispel the idea with logic: 'But how of Cawdor? the thane of

Cawdor lives.' Instead of replying, however, the witches vanish. As a result, temptation is presented as a force that need not even engage with logic to be effective.

Theme/Paragraph Two: Shakespeare in this passage presents temptation as a weapon of womanhood – a form of sexualised persuasion designed to entrap men.

- In this passage, not only do Lady Macbeth's comments draw attention to her gender, but they also have distinct sexual undertones. When trying to convince Macbeth to keep his word, she claims that, in order to keep a promise, she would kill a baby nursing – 'giv[ing] suck' – at her breast: she claims she would have 'plucked [her] nipple from his boneless gums / and dashed the brains out, had I so sworn.' Taken on a literal level, the imagery of infanticide firmly establishes a sense of malevolent womanhood.[3] However, perhaps more interesting are the sexual undertones: when viewed through a Freudian lens, the phrase 'given suck' might call to mind oral sex, whereas the image of 'boneless gums' is arguably reminiscent of a vagina. [*AO1 for advancing the argument with a judiciously selected quote; AO2 for the close analysis of the language*].
- Temptation – particularly sexual temptation – would have been commonly understood by Elizabethan and early Jacobean audiences as a tool used by women to exert control over men. This would have been informed in no small part by contemporary portrayals of Adam and Eve. At the time, Eve was often

portrayed as a seductress, leading Adam astray with
her sexuality. Indeed, shortly before this passage,
Lady Macbeth tells Macbeth to 'Look like th'
innocent flower, / But be the serpent under 't.' This
exhortation to emulate the very entity ('the serpent')
that seduced Eve further casts Lady Macbeth as a
sexual temptress in the mould of Eve. [*AO2 for the
close analysis of the language; AO3 for placing the
play in a cultural, literary, and historical context*].

Theme/Paragraph Three: Temptation is presented as a tool that endows the individual wielding it with rhetorical prowess and heightened confidence.

- Perhaps the most striking thing about Lady Macbeth's
  speech here is her rhetorical prowess: the desire to
  tempt Macbeth has brought out an almost
  supernatural eloquence in her. Take, for instance,
  Lady Macbeth's observation that, although time and
  place have aligned, Macbeth is failing to act: 'They
  have made themselves and that their fitness now /
  Does unmake you.' Lady Macbeth here is more than
  just chastising Macbeth for choking. By personifying
  time and space – 'they have made themselves' – Lady
  Macbeth gives them a tangibility that impresses on
  Macbeth the momentousness of the opportunity: time
  and space themselves have deigned to play a
  supporting cast in their plans. Moreover, the phrase
  'Does unmake you' casts the failure to act as an
  existential threat: his very self will be unmade by
  inaction.[4] [*AO1 for advancing the argument with a*

judiciously selected quote; AO2 for the close analysis of the language].

- *Elsewhere in the play*: It is no coincidence that the witches – the equivocating trio that 'lies like truth' – also share this silver-tongued prowess. However, Macbeth's rhetoric is also heightened when he turns his hand to tempting others: in Act 3 Scene 1, he tempts the would-be murderers of Banquo with the promise that following through with the murder would curry favour, using a cleverly inverted trochaic foot at the start of the line to create emphasis: 'Grapples you to the heart and love of us.' [*AO2 for the close analysis of the language*].

Conclusion

Again, we have put together a meaty essay; however, I once more have an extra point I want to acknowledge – the fact that temptation only seems to sway those with outsized ambitions and insecurities in the first place. As a result, I shall integrate it into the conclusion, while also scoring some final AO3 points while I'm at it:

"Throughout the play, temptation is presented as an almost supernatural force that inspires eloquence in those wielding it, and compels those on its receiving end. The idea of temptation being induced by supernatural eloquence would have brought to mind in Shakespeare's audience the Sirens from Homer's Greek epic, *The Odyssey*, a text that was well known at the time. However, whereas the Sirens' song drove any given listener mad with desire, temptation does not exist in a vacuum in *Macbeth*.[5] Instead, it preys on those with insecurities and ambitions. This explains why Banquo is far more inoculated to the witches' words, whereas Macbeth is susceptible to as simple a tactic as his wife calling into question his manhood: 'you were a man.'"

Glamis Castle in Scotland. Although it has a hall named after Duncan, the murder in the play actually takes place at Macbeth's castle in Inverness.

At this point in the play, Duncan has been murdered and an oblivious Macduff has arrived at Macbeth's home.

PORTER
'Faith sir, we were carousing till the
second cock: and drink, sir, is a great
provoker of three things.

MACDUFF
What three things does drink especially provoke?

PORTER
Marry, sir, nose-painting, sleep, and
urine. Lechery, sir, it provokes, and unprovokes;
it provokes the desire, but it takes
away the performance: therefore, much drink
may be said to be an equivocator with lechery:
it makes him, and it mars him; it sets
him on, and it takes him off; it persuades him,
and disheartens him; makes him stand to, and

not stand to; in conclusion, equivocates him
in a sleep, and, giving him the lie, leaves him.

**Starting with this passage, how does
Shakespeare use humour in *Macbeth*?**

Write about:

**• how Shakespeare presents humour in this
extract**

**• how Shakespeare presents humour in the
play as a whole**

Introduction

"Whereas in Ancient Greek tragedy humour and
tragedy were ring-fenced, the Elizabethan and
Jacobean eras saw a breakdown in these conventions, as
evidenced by the Fool in *King Lear* and *Hamlet*'s
Gravediggers.[1] The Porter – *Macbeth*'s comedic cameo
part – demonstrates how Shakespeare uses comedy to
dispel and relieve tension; however, Shakespeare also
uses humour to echo and obliquely explore more
serious themes in the play."

**Theme/Paragraph One: By having the Porter
deploy bawdy humour as he talks at length about
alcohol's impact on men's sexual organs, Shakespeare uses comedy to echo other motifs: namely,**

the macabre sexuality of the witches and Macbeth's impotence.

- In response to Macduff's humouring question, the Porter explores in depth the impact of alcohol on men's sexual performance – more specifically, he describes how it triggers sexual arousal, yet induces erectile dysfunction: 'makes him stand to, and / not stand to.' Shakespeare, using 'not stand to' as a euphemism for the failure to achieve an erection, enhances the punch line with the line break just beforehand, cleverly using form to enhance the meaning. [*AO1 for advancing the argument with a judiciously selected quote; AO2 for the close analysis of the language and for discussing how form shapes meaning*].

- *Elsewhere in the play*: Shakespeare is using humour here as a tactic to echo other motifs and concerns that are central to the play. More specifically, the Porter's use of bawdy humour functions to echo the far more sinister bawdiness of the witches: their remarks in Act 1, for example, bring to mind oral sex: 'in her lap, / And munch'd, and munch'd.' As a result of this, the Porter's comedy functions to keep the influence of the witches alive in the audience's imagination.

- *Elsewhere in the play*: It might also be noted that the specific theme of impotence in this comedic patter echoes Macbeth's earlier spell of impotence: namely, his initial inability (which he eventually overcomes) to carry out the murder of Duncan. The phallic nature of the weapon he uses, the dagger, further emphasises this echo. Again, the comedy functions to keep certain other events at the fore of the audience's mind.

Theme/Paragraph Two: The comedy in this passage, by invoking equivocation, shines a light on the idea of equivocation that appears throughout the play, and invites us to see it in a fresh light.

- The Porter, while discussing alcohol, noticeably uses the word 'equivocator' to describe its effect upon the libido: 'drink / may be said to be an equivocator with lechery.' The passage also ends with another reference to equivocation: the Porter suggests that alcohol induces a kind of equivocal sleep that arouses, yet ultimately fails to satisfy: it 'equivocates him / in a sleep, and, giving him the lie, leaves him.' The play on 'lie' packs a comedic punch. Equivocation refers to a rhetorical technique in which someone uses ambiguous language in order to mislead. As a result, 'lie' refers not only to the sleep alcohol encourages, but also the way it misleads the libido. [*AO1 for advancing the argument with a judiciously selected quote; AO2 for the close analysis of the language*].

- *Elsewhere in the play*: By deploying equivocation in a comedic context, however, Shakespeare is also asking the audience to see the darkly humorous side of the events that arise from the witches' equivocations. Time and again, Macbeth describes the witches' language as equivocal ('the equivocation / Of the fiend that lies like truth'). However, the way that perhaps their most famous equivocation pans out – they promise that Macbeth will survive until Birnam Woods comes to the castle; he is then defeated when the encroaching army clad themselves in the branches of said woods – does indeed smack of absurdist comedy. King Macbeth is brought down by a ludicrous loophole.

Theme/Paragraph Three: Shakespeare uses the Porter's humour here as a form of comic relief, granting the audience some reprieve from the horrors of the previous scene.

- The timing of the Porter's 'carousing' appearance in the play is of utmost importance: the audience has just endured the trauma of the regicidal sequence that immediately preceded it, and appears before the grotesqueries that ensue once Duncan's body is found. By opting to makes this structural choice, Shakespeare is using humour to relieve the tension and offer the audience some respite. [AO2 *for discussing how structure shapes meaning*].

- However, even as Shakespeare seeks to relieve tension, he still litters the speech with language that brings to mind the monstrousness of what has unfolded. While the Porter's reference to 'nose painting' is a playful nod to the way that alcohol bursts blood vessels in the nose, it still subtly reminds the audience of the much more serious bloodshed in the previous scene. Moreover, the playful reference to alcoholic slumber calls to mind not just Duncan's eternal sleep, but also the drug induced sleep of his guards.

- Shakespeare's audience would have understood this passage as a parody of a medieval morality play, *The Harrowing of Hell*, in which Christ attempts to gain entry to hell, but is waylaid by the Porter. As a result, while the parodic element would have enhanced the comic relief for the audience, the fact it was alluding to a deeply serious play would have emphasised the fact that this sequence cannot be disentangled from the serious events preceding and proceeding it. [AO3 *for placing the play in a literary-historical context*].

Conclusion

At this point, the essay has jumped through the exam board's assessment objectives pretty thoroughly. As a result, I intend to finish with a flourish that focuses on AO1 marks.

"Macbeth, in Act 5 Scene 5, describes the play's proceedings as 'a tale / Told by an idiot, full of sound and fury, / Signifying nothing.' If the tale is told by an idiot, it is one in the mould of Lear's sardonic fool, and the yarn he has spun is a perfect blend of dark tragedy and absurdist gallows humour. Indeed, as evidenced by this Porter scene, even when the play does attempt a full-blown comedic sequence, such a sequence does not simply just keep an eye on the play's serious events. Rather, it strives to alter the audience's perception of those events."

A statue of Shakespeare in Stratford-upon-Avon, the town in which he was born.

At this point in the play, Macbeth and Lady Macbeth have just ascended to the throne.

BANQUO
Thou hast it now: king, Cawdor, Glamis, all,
As the weird women promised, and, I fear,
Thou play'dst most foully for't: yet it was said
It should not stand in thy posterity,
But that myself should be the root and father
Of many kings. If there come truth from them—
As upon thee, Macbeth, their speeches shine—
Why, by the verities on thee made good,
May they not be my oracles as well,
And set me up in hope? But hush! no more.
Sennet sounded. Enter MACBETH, as king, LADY
MACBETH, as queen, LENNOX, ROSS, Lords,
Ladies, and Attendants
MACBETH
Here's our chief guest.

LADY MACBETH

If he had been forgotten,
It had been as a gap in our great feast,
And all-thing unbecoming.

Starting with this extract, discuss the extent to which Banquo is presented as a heroic character.

Write about:

• **how Shakespeare presents Banquo as a heroic character in this extract**

• **how Shakespeare presents Banquo as a heroic character in the play as a whole**

Introduction

The same old formula: I am starting with an AO3 titbit of context, then following up with some indication of the themes I'm planning to throw down.

"Whereas in Greek tragedies the heroes were invariably royal, Shakespeare's *Macbeth* presents a more complicated picture: the drama revolves around an impostor King (Macbeth) and his friend (Banquo) who, while not himself royal, winds up the progenitor of royalty. Banquo first appears, alongside Macbeth, as a wartime hero, and his heroic status is compounded by his tragic death; however, his heroism arguably pales in

comparison to Macduff's, the individual who
eventually takes down Macbeth."

Theme/Paragraph One: The expressing of ambition might subvert Banquo heroic status, as it puts him in the same league as Macbeth. However, his hopes are not for himself, but for his descendants, which suggests that his desires are less selfish.

- Banquo ponders on whether, since the witches have been right about Macbeth, they might have been correct in their prediction about his progeny being royalty: 'May they not be my oracles as well, / and set me up in hope?' Arguably, Banquo, by harbouring royal ambitions, is falling into the same trap as Macbeth, thereby detracting from his heroic potential; indeed, the phrase 'my oracles' might seem an unduly cordial label for the malevolent witches. [AO1 *for advancing the argument with a judiciously selected quote; AO2 for the close analysis of the language*].

- However, it must be added that Banquo's ambitions are intrinsically less selfish: his 'hope' is for his descendants, not himself. Moreover, given that he understands that Macbeth likely committed regicide ('Thou play'dst most foully for't'), his desire to see Macbeth replaced might be more noble: he wishes to see the usurper usurped. Finally, the way he cuts off his own meditation on ambition as Macbeth approaches ('But hush! no more') could contain a double meaning. Unlike Macbeth's ambition, which 'o'erleaps itself,' Banquo's is eminently controllable –

something he can simply 'hush.' [*AO1 for advancing the argument with a judiciously selected quote; AO2 for the close analysis of the language*].

- *Elsewhere in the play*. Certainly, this assessment tallies with their initial reaction to the witches in Act 1, at which point Banquo kept a level head in the face of the witches' predictions, whereas Macbeth 'start[s]... and seem[s] to fear.'

Theme/Paragraph Two: Banquo's slowness to act on his suspicions can, on one hand, be seen as a character flaw that in some senses elevates him to the status tragic hero. On the other hand, it could arguably be seen to relegate him to the status of victim.

- It is striking here that, although Banquo understands that Macbeth 'playd'st most foully' for the crown, he does not choose to act against him, or indeed even put up his guard. Aristotle, a seminal Greek philosopher, argued that the key marker of a tragic hero was a fatal character flaw that leads to their downfall (known as a *hamartia*).[1] Since Aristotle was widely read in Jacobean England, Shakespeare's audience would have been alert to the fact that Banquo's inertia – as well as perhaps his desire to still see the good in Macbeth – marked him out as a tragic hero. After all, by failing to act, he leaves himself a lamb to Macbeth's slaughter in the scene that follows. [*AO1 for advancing the argument with a judiciously selected quote; AO3 for placing the play in a cultural, literary, and historical context*].

- However, when it comes to a modern audience for whom heroism is more often associated with infallibility and triumph, this very same trait in Banquo might cause him to be construed as a victim instead. Indeed, by a modern audience's standards, Macduff is far more likely to fit the bill of a hero, given his heroic storming of Dunsinane castle and slaying of Macbeth in the play's final act.

Theme/Paragraph Three: The use of stagecraft gives Banquo an air of heroism, since he is placed on stage here as a leading man.

- The stagecraft during this passage in the play lends Banquo a gravitas that boosts his claim to heroic status. This soliloquy is the opening speech of Act 3, a structural choice that affords his words special emphasis and gives his soliloquy the temporary air of a leading man. Furthermore, when Macbeth and his extensive entourage – 'LADY MACBETH, as queen, LENNOX, ROSS, Lords, Ladies, and Attendants' – enter at the close of Banquo's soliloquy, it creates a tableau in which the solitary Banquo is stacked up against an intimidating array of bodies, and which thus visually casts Banquo as the antihero's (Macbeth's) opposite number. [AO2 *for discussing how structure shapes meaning*].
- *Elsewhere in the play*: Stagecraft is also used to emphasise Banquo's heroic status when his ghost reappears in Act 3 Scene 4. In that scene, Lennox invites to Macbeth to sit: 'May't please your highness sit.' However, it is Banquo's ghost who in fact then places himself on Macbeth's seat, implicitly

suggesting that he is the entity who ought to be addressed as 'your highness.' The use of elision in 'may't' could subtly reflect that Banquo is still, however, absent in flesh and blood.[2] [*AO2 for the close analysis of the language*].

Theme/Paragraph Four: Banquo's significance is affirmed by his outsized presence in Macbeth and Lady Macbeth's minds.

- As Macbeth and Lady Macbeth set eyes on Banquo, both make comments that seek to elevate Banquo and emphasise his significance: Macbeth refers to him 'as our chief guest' and Lady Macbeth, not to be undone, claims that Banquo's absence would be 'a gap in our feast' and 'unbecoming.' While at first glance the pair appear simply to be heaping praise on Banquo, the subtext is plain: they consider him an outsized threat to their reign – an individual with the potential to bring about their 'unbecoming.' Again, this anxiety towards Banquo from the play's antiheroes logically casts him as their mirror image: the hero. [*AO1 for advancing the argument with a judiciously selected quote; AO2 for the close analysis of the language*].
- *Elsewhere in the play*. Although, during the ghost sequence, Banquo most certainly has an outsized presence in Macbeth's mind, this is not necessarily true for much of the play. In the first couple of Acts, Duncan is front and centre of Macbeth and Lady Macbeth's minds. Moreover, once Banquo's ghost departs, Macbeth and Lady Macbeth both turn their attention to other individuals.

Conclusion

This essay has ambitiously tackled four hefty paragraphs, and I am content that we have scored almost every mark that is up for grabs. However, to play it safe, I will once again invoke historical context as I wrap things up, just to ensure that no AO3 marks slip through the cracks:

"The first time Banquo is mentioned in the play, he is described, alongside Macbeth, as being like a 'lion' on the battlefield against Macdonwald, thereby setting both up as potential heroes. However, whereas Macbeth heads down a dark path, Banquo's steadfast morality allows him to still stake claim to heroic status. It might also be noted that King James I – who ascended to the throne in 1603 – was understood at the time to be a descendent of Banquo's. This would have enhanced Banquo's aura of heroism to Shakespeare's audience, since it would have confirmed the notion that Banquo was indeed the progenitor of royalty."

At this point in the play, Macbeth has just learned that Macduff has left the country.

MACBETH
Fled to England!
LENNOX
Ay, my good lord.
MACBETH
Time, thou anticipatest my dread exploits:
The flighty purpose never is o'ertook
Unless the deed go with it; from this moment
The very firstlings of my heart shall be
The firstlings of my hand. And even now,
To crown my thoughts with acts, be it thought and
    done:
The castle of Macduff I will surprise;
Seize upon Fife; give to the edge o' the sword
His wife, his babes, and all unfortunate souls
That trace him in his line. No boasting like a fool;

This deed I'll do before this purpose cool.
But no more sights!--Where are these gentlemen?
Come, bring me where they are.

Starting with this passage, discuss how far you think Shakespeare presents Macbeth as a leader.

Write about:

• **how Shakespeare presents Macbeth as a leader in this extract**

• **how Shakespeare presents Macbeth as a leader in the play as a whole**

Introduction

Once again, I have opted to go for the one-two punch of an AO3 point, followed quickly by thematic comments that lay the foundation for AO1 point scoring:

"In 1606, the year *Macbeth* was first performed, concerns about leadership were at the forefront of the public mind: three years earlier, Elizabeth I had died and was replaced by James I. However, whereas Elizabeth died of natural causes, *Macbeth* dramatises a shift in monarchical power to Macbeth after he commits the act of regicide. Yet while Macbeth is ironically led into this seizing of leadership by others (namely, the witches and Lady

Macbeth), he does begin to embody decisiveness once on the throne."

Theme/Paragraph One: In this passage, Macbeth, on hearing that Macduff has fled to England, embodies decisive action – a key leadership trait – in ordering the murder of Macduff's family.

- Just prior to this passage, Macbeth has learned from the witches that he ought to be wary of Macduff, and this is confirmed by the news that he has 'fled to England,' where Duncan's son, Malcolm, is in exile. As a result, his decision to strike the first blow against Macduff – that is, by targeting 'his wife, his babes' – can be construed as a savvy move of a leader looking to reconcile power. [*AO1 for advancing the argument with a judiciously selected quote*].

- Indeed, Macbeth is quick to articulate his decisive leadership mentality: 'The very firstling of my heart shall be / The firstlings of my hand.' The quick communication between 'heart' and 'hand' emphasises the rapidity of his decision making, whereas the word 'firstling' invites us to consider how he is now fully taking on the role of the nation's first and ultimate decision-maker. Moreover, the trochaic words – 'very,' 'firstlings' – create a falling cadence that emulates the swift handing-down of his verdict.[1] [*AO2 for the close analysis of the language*].

- *Elsewhere in the play*: His decisive leadership here stands in stark contrast to his prevarications just prior to his slaying of Duncan. At that point, he vacillated between cultivating his ambitions, and attempting to nix the whole affair: 'We will proceed no further in this business.'

Theme/Paragraph Two: Although Macbeth appears to be taking the lead in this passage, it is clear he lacks the morality one traditionally considers a prerequisite of effective leadership.

- Earlier in this scene, the witches hail Macbeth as 'something wicked,' and this seems to be borne out in this passage, in which Macbeth callously orders the murder of Macduff's 'wife, his babes' and any 'unfortunate souls / who trace [Macduff] in his line.' While the word 'unfortunate' gives hope of a shred of empathy in Macbeth, it is undercut by his monstrous haste. He matter-of-factly states he wishes to carry this out 'before this purpose cool:' he is intentionally trying to short-circuit and 'cool' any regret that could conceivably kick in.

- Looking again at Macbeth's claim to make the 'firstling of [his] heart' into 'the firstlings of my hand,' one might see an irony. The phraseology evokes the idiom of wearing one's heart upon their sleeve. However, Macbeth is in fact behaving with a shocking lack of emotion. [AO2 *for the close analysis of the language*].

- *Elsewhere in the play*: Macbeth time and again exhibits his moral failings. Perhaps most striking is his orchestration of Banquo's murder in the previous act. Given the adherence to Christian orthodoxy at the time, Shakespeare's audience would undoubtedly have construed these moral failings as failings of leadership. Instead, they would have favoured the moral leadership embodied by *King Lear*'s Cordelia, whose army marches for 'love, dear love.'[2] [*AO3 for placing the text in a literary-historical context*].

Theme/Paragraph Three: While it has been argued that Macbeth takes the lead in this passage, it ought to be noted that, in a sense, he is still dancing to the witches' tune. Indeed, it is surely the witches, not Macbeth, who play the part of master puppeteer

- Macbeth here meditates that time seems to anticipate his plans: 'Time, thou anticipatest my dread exploits.' However, it is not time that anticipates his 'dread exploits;' rather, it is the witches. In fact, they are directly causing his exploits. While the decision to attack Macduff's terrain superficially seems to be Macbeth's own – the word 'I' in 'the castle of Macduff I will surprise' lending a veneer of agency – one is left doubtful whether he would have chosen this course of action if not for the witches' warning. Moreover, the fact this speech comes at the end of the scene gives the structural impression that he is not leading, but following. [*AO1 for advancing the argument with a judiciously selected quote; AO2 for the close analysis of the language and for discussing how structure shapes meaning*].

- *Elsewhere in the play*: This passage is indicative of a wider pattern: the witches take dominion over Macbeth's life from the very start of the play, leading him down the path to regicide with their predictions. Yet it is not just the witches who are seen leading the pliable Macbeth. Lady Macbeth does so, too, in the run-up to Duncan's murder: she is the one who galvanizes Macbeth and guides his dagger.

Conclusion

I have one final point I want to bring in: the fact that, at least temporarily, King Macbeth is able to induce loyalty in his men. As a result, I have opted to cover that base, while adding in one last contextual nod to *Hamlet* for good measure on the AO3 front.

"In this passage, the decisive Macbeth stands in stark contrast with the likes of Hamlet: there is no 'to be or not to be,' but simply a 'be it thought and done.'[3] Indeed, that Lennox defers to Macbeth here – 'ay my good lord' – imbues him with the gravitas of a leader. However, while Macbeth is presented as a leader through the obedience he commands in his men, this proves short-lived: his failings in moral leadership induces them all – including Lenox – to eventually abandon ship. The fact that the only loyalist left by the end of the play is the demonically-named 'Seyton' is not only a testament to Macbeth's lapsed leadership, but also a reminder of the play's true powerbrokers: the 'weird sisters.'"

Shakespeare's home in Stratford-upon-Avon

A t this point in the play, enemy forces are storming King Macbeth's castle.

LADY MACBETH

Yet here's a spot.

DOCTOR

Hark! she speaks: I will set down what comes from
her, to satisfy my remembrance the more strongly.

LADY MACBETH

Out, damned spot! out, I say!–One: two: why,
then, 'tis time to do't. –Hell is murky! –Fie, my
lord, fie! a soldier, and afeard? What need we
fear who knows it, when none can call our power to
account? –Yet who would have thought the old man
to have had so much blood in him.

DOCTOR

Do you mark that?

LADY MACBETH

The thane of Fife had a wife: where is she now? –

What, will these hands ne'er be clean? –No more o'
that, my lord, no more o' that: you mar all with'
this starting.
Doctor
Go to, go to; you have known what you should not.

**Starting with this extract, how does
Shakespeare present Lady Macbeth as a
woman who is losing control.**

Write about:

• **how Shakespeare presents Lady Macbeth
as losing control in this extract**

• **how Shakespeare presents Lady Macbeth
as losing control in the play as a whole**

Introduction

"Although Queen Elizabeth, the head of state till 1603,
was an archetype of a woman in control, the popular
imagination was also littered with women losing their
grip on sanity; chief among them, the suicidal Ophelia
from Shakespeare's *Hamlet*. Lady Macbeth straddles
the two archetypes: she is, in the play's earlier stages,
the model of composure; but – as evidenced by this
passage – she is later plagued with hallucinations and
delusions of grandeur that are testament to her loss of
control."

Theme/Paragraph One: Shakespeare, by having Lady Macbeth spill the details of her crimes, clearly communicates her slackening grip on sanity: she is incriminating herself.

- As she unleashes her stream of consciousness, Lady Macbeth – seemingly oblivious to the risks of doing so – all but confesses to the heinous crimes she and Macbeth have committed. Although Duncan is not mentioned by name, the invocation of his murder is unmistakable: Lady Macbeth states that she had not 'thought the old man / to have had so much blood in him.' The informal way she refers to Duncan as 'the old man,' as though not fully cognizant of the fact she is in company, serves only to redouble the impression of deteriorating mental alacrity. [*AO1 for advancing the argument with a judiciously selected quote; AO2 for the close analysis of the language*].

- Moreover, the comment that 'the thane of Fife had a wife' not only strongly hints at her responsibility for Macduff's wife's murder, but also, through the internal rhyme on 'Fife' and 'wife,' gives the passage a nursery rhyme feel that hints at her regressing mental state. For Shakespeare's audience, this motif of a secret coup spilling into public view might have reminded them of Francis Throkmorton's 1584 plot to overthrow Queen Elizabeth and restore Catholicism, which Throkmorton confessed to under torture. [*AO3 for placing the text in a historical context*].

- *Elsewhere in the play*: Her loose lipped behaviour contrasts with earlier in the play, when the very-much-in control Lady Macbeth had previously been intently focused on covering up her crimes: she artfully frames Duncan's guards and washes away evidence of her crime.

Theme/Paragraph Two: Through her hallucinations, it is suggested that Lady Macbeth has lost her grip on reality. Indeed, in this sequence, Lady Macbeth is in a kind of sleep-walking state, further hinting at her lack of control: her body and mouth are active without her knowledge or consent.

- Lady Macbeth's opening comment in this passage – 'yet here's a spot' – immediately points to her hallucinatory state: she is imagining a spot of Duncan's blood on her palm that in fact is not there. By placing this phrase at the start of this passage, Shakespeare has it structurally function as a kind of epigraph in miniature, preparing the audience for the fact that this passage will delve into Lady Macbeth's hallucinatory state of mind. Indeed, the conceit is pursued when Lady Macbeth next talks: 'Out, damned spot! out, I say!' – the three consecutive spondaic feet hinting at an unhinged patter of speech that reflects the unhinged mental state. [*AO1 for advancing the argument with a judiciously selected quote; AO2 for the close analysis of the language*].
- Interestingly, the hallucination is not just visual; it is olfactory: 'Here's the smell of the blood still' This demonstrates that her hallucinatory madness has colonized multiple of her senses.
- *Elsewhere in the play*: There is a good deal of irony in the fact that, earlier in the play, Macbeth had been

hallucinating – as evidenced by the ghost of Banquo, which only Macbeth can see – and Lady Macbeth had scolded him for his inability to keep a handle on himself. However, she is now the one hallucinating, an indication that she is the one who has lost control.

Theme/Paragraph Three: Lady Macbeth's grandiose claim that she is above reproach, and immune from being held to account, in fact ironically displays her frailty: she has a burning need to reassure herself of her safety.

- In the face of her guilt-ridden hallucination, Lady Macbeth asserts that she does not 'need [to] fear' because 'none can call our power to account' – an attempt to reassure herself that only serves to highlight her anxiety. When Lady Macbeth then cuts short her guilty monologue with 'No more o' that, my lord, no more o' that,' she is again adopting the regal position of being above the law to delude herself that she is still in control. Shakespeare's audience would have been familiar with the concept of the Divine Rights of Kings – the concept that the monarch was imbued with authority from God – and it appears as if Lady Macbeth is almost trying to insulate herself by invoking her theoretical authority. [*AO1 for advancing the argument with a judiciously selected quote*]
- *Elsewhere in the play*: However, the absurdity of the claim that being a royal will protect her from calamity is revealed by her own actions earlier in the play.

Duncan's royal status did nothing to protect him from Lady Macbeth's regicidal machinations.

Theme/Paragraph Four: The erratic style of Lady Macbeth's speech here, as well as its content, further illustrate her lack of control.

- In this passage, Lady Macbeth rapidly shifts between emotions – from guilt, to defiance, to hysterical humour (as mentioned, 'The Thane of Fife had a wife' has an unhinged comical nature to it). Furthermore, the punctuation indicates her frantic state of mind: the speech is littered with question marks, commas, and dashes: 'One: two: why, / then, 'tis time to do't. – Hell is murky!–Fie, my / lord, fie!' Her lack of control over her speech – both in terms of the erratic content and the form – mirrors her lack of control over her emotions. Its style is reminiscent of Edgar's in *King Lear* – a character who talks in such a way to intentionally create the impression of madness. [AO2 *for the close analysis of the language and for discussing how form shapes meaning*].
- *Elsewhere in the play*: This contrasts with her 'unsex me here' speech earlier in the play which is clear, flowing, and logical, thereby demonstrating her increasing loss of control at the twilight of the play.

Conclusion

"In this passage, it is clear that Lady Macbeth has 'eaten of the insane root' invoked by Banquo at the play's start: the once Machiavellian femme fatale has been reduced to the sexist seventeenth century archetype of a woman struck with womb madness.[1] However, while it is irrefutable that Lady Macbeth's mental clarity has deteriorated as a result of her guilt, it should also be acknowledged that even at the start of the play she had ceded a degree of control of her sanity – that is, to the mania of ambition."

Street art rendering of Shakespeare in London

ENDNOTES

ESSAY PLAN ONE

1. To be ambivalent is to have mixed feelings about something or someone.
2. Faust is an individual from German myth who, in exchange for magical abilities, agrees to hand over his soul to the devil. As a result, the word "Faustian" is now used to describe someone engaged in a sordid exchange in which they compromise themselves morally.
3. The word "Freudian" refers to the father of psychoanalysis, Sigmund Freud (1856 – 1939). His works explore the hidden sexual motivations that drive human beings. When we are doing a Freudian reading of a text, we are looking for the hidden sexual imagery – imagery that perhaps even the author themselves had not realised had possessed sexual undertones.
4. I suspect you are asking: what are inverted spondaic feet? Let me explain from the top.

    Shakespeare's plays are almost entirely written in *iambic pentameter*. An iamb is a metrical foot in which the emphasis is on the second syllable, and tends to sound more like natural speech. A pentameter is when there are five metrical feet in a line.

    It is often easiest to illustrate with an example. If we take the fifth line of Macbeth's speech, and use bold font to represent the stressed syllables, plus a vertical bar to indicate the end of each metrical foot, it will look like this: 'Can**not** | be **ill**, | can**not** | be **good**: | if **ill**.' Since there are five metrical feet here, all iambic, it is rendered in iambic pentameter.

    A trochee, on the other hand, is a metrical foot in which the emphasis is on the first syllable, and tends to sound more unnatural. To illustrate, let us look at the sixth line from this extract, and mark out the stresses on syllables: 'Why **hath** | it **giv** | en **me** | **earn**est | of succ | **ess**.' As you can see, while the first three feet are iambs, the fourth is in fact a trochee. Since Shakespeare does not usually use trochees, we would call this an *inverted* trochaic foot: he is inverting how he usually does things.

    But that's not the only odd thing in this line. You'll notice that the fifth foot has no stress on either syllable. This is known as a pyrrhic foot. And then there's that extra stressed syllable at the end. This is known as a *stressed hyperbeat* or a *masculine ending*. (If it had been an unstressed syllable, it would have been an *unstressed hyperbeat* or a *feminine ending*).

    So, finally, what is a spondee? This is when both syllables in a metrical foot are stressed. To illustrate, let's look at the tenth line in this extract: 'And **make** | **my seat** | ed **heart** | **knock at** | **my ribs**.' As you can see, the second, fourth and fifth feet are all spondees. As a result, we describe them as inverted spondaic feet.

5. I have chosen to use the phrase Jacobean audience – as opposed to Elizabethan audience – because Macbeth was first performed in 1606, at which point King James I had replaced Elizabeth I on the throne (Elizabeth died in 1603).

6. Litotes is a rhetorical device in which the speaker is deliberately understating something. To illustrate, it's like when someone says "hey, this pizza isn't bad" as a way of saying: "this pizza is amazing!"

7. An epigraph is a short quote at the beginning of a work of literature that hints at the themes and concepts that will be discussed.

8. Horatio is Hamlet's close friend in Shakespeare's most famous tragedy, *Hamlet*.

9. If something is ubiquitous, it means it is everywhere.

ESSAY PLAN TWO

1. Dramatis Personae is a Latin phrase and refers to the characters who appear in a play or novel.

ESSAY PLAN THREE

1. Genesis is a book in the Old Testament of the Bible. Adam and Eve – the first two humans beings – live in the paradisal Garden of Eden. However, the devil, disguised as a snake, convinces Eve to eat an apple from the Tree of Knowledge – something that God had expressly forbidden. Eve then persuades Adam to eat the forbidden fruit, too. As a result, God boots both of them out of Eden.

2. Regicide refers to the act of killing a king!

3. Infanticide refers to the killing of an infant.

4. An existential threat is something that threatens your existence.

5. In *The Odyssey*, the Sirens were mythical creatures who inhabited an island and whose alluring song would induce such wild temptation in the sailors attempting to pass by that the sailors would end up shipwrecked on the rocky coast.

ESSAY PLAN FOUR

1. In King Lear – a tragedy perhaps even more bleak than *Macbeth* – Lear is accompanied for much of the play by his jester, the Fool. The Fool, however, is no intellectual lightweight. On the contrary, he is verbally

erudite, and frequently makes ironic and cutting remarks that show him to be more than just a comedic sideshow.

In *Hamlet*, the Gravediggers play a smaller part, but again represent comedic characters who are also deeply intelligent and ironic.

ESSAY PLAN FIVE

1. This idea is introduced in Aristotle's *Poetics*, in which he outlines the nature of tragedy.
2. Elision is when you remove a syllable or a sound from a word, and is usually signified by an apostrophe replacing the missing syllable. We use elision all the time in present-day English – for example, 'let's' and 'I'm'.

ESSAY PLAN SIX

1. You'll notice here that I'm talking about trochaic words as opposed to trochaic feet. Let me explain.

   First off, let's take a look at the line in question, and use bold font to represent the stressed syllables, plus a vertical bar to indicate the end of each metrical foot: 'The **ve** | ry **first** | lings **of** | my **heart** | shall **be**.' As you can see, the stress is on the second syllable in every single foot, meaning that the line is written in iambic pentameter.

   However, the words 'very' and 'firstlings,' when taken in isolation, are trochees: '**ve**ry' '**first**lings.' As a result, what we have are trochaic words broken over iambic feet. The result is a tension between the rising rhythm of the iambic pentameter, and the falling rhythm of these trochaic words.
2. In *King Lear*, Cordelia – the daughter Lear spurns at the start of the play – marches the French army to face-down her two sisters, Goneril and Regan, because these sisters have abandoned and abused their father.
3. The drama of *Hamlet* revolves around Hamlet trying to convince himself to act against his uncle Claudius – because Claudius killed Hamlet's father in order to steal the throne. As a result, the line 'to be or not to be' can be read as Hamlet paining over whether to act.

ESSAY PLAN SEVEN

1. In Shakespeare's time, there was a sexist notion that a woman's womb could induce madness.

AFTERWORD

To keep up to date with Accolade Press, visit https://
accoladetuition.com/accolade-press. You can also join our
private Facebook group (where our authors share resources and
guidance) by visiting the following link: https://rcl.ink/DME.

Printed in Great Britain
by Amazon